MyReportLinks.com Books

Tools   Search   Notes   Discuss

STATES

MAINE

A MyReportLinks.com Book

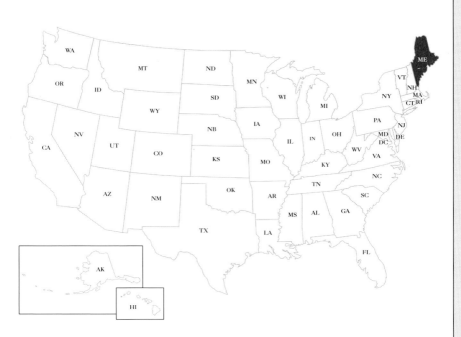

Amy Graham

MyReportLinks.com Books

 an imprint of
Enslow Publishers, Inc.
Box 398, 40 Industrial Road
Berkeley Heights, NJ 07922
USA

To my grandmothers, daughters of Maine

MyReportLinks.com Books, an imprint of Enslow Publishers, Inc.

Copyright © 2002 by Enslow Publishers, Inc.

All rights reserved.

No part of this book may be reproduced by any means without the written permission of the publisher.

Library of Congress Cataloging-in-Publication Data

Graham, Amy.
  Maine / Amy Graham.
      p. cm. — (States)
Includes bibliographical references and index.
Summary: Discusses the highlights, land and climate, economy, government, and history of the state of Maine.
  ISBN 0-7660-5017-3
  1. Maine—Juvenile literature. [1. Maine.] I. Title. II. States (Series : Berkeley Heights, N.J.)
  F19.3 .G73 2002
  974.1—dc21
                                                          2001004312

Printed in the United States of America

10 9 8 7 6 5 4 3 2 1

To Our Readers:
Through the purchase of this book, you and your library gain access to the Report Links that specifically back up this book.
The Publisher will provide access to the Report Links that back up this book and will keep these Report Links up to date on www.myreportlinks.com for three years from the book's first publication date.
We have done our best to make sure all Internet addresses in this book were active and appropriate when we went to press. However, the author and the Publisher have no control over, and assume no liability for, the material available on those Internet sites or on other Web sites they may link to.
The usage of the MyReportLinks.com Books Web site is subject to the terms and conditions stated on the Usage Policy Statement on www.myreportlinks.com.
In the future, a password may be required to access the Report Links that back up this book. The password is found on the bottom of page 4 of this book.
Any comments or suggestions can be sent by e-mail to comments@myreportlinks.com or to the address on the back cover.

Photo Credits: © Corel Corporation, pp. 3, 10, 14, 20, 21, 22, 23, 32; © 1999 PhotoDisc, Inc., p. 33; Courtesy of Acadia National Park, p. 12; Courtesy of Lighthousegetaway.com, p. 44; Courtesy of MtKatahdin.com, p. 13; Courtesy of MyReportLinks.com Books, p. 4; Courtesy of National Park Service, p. 43; Courtesy of Skimaine.com, p. 29; Courtesy of the Canadian Heritage Rivers System, p. 18; Courtesy of The Maine Attraction, p. 11; Courtesy of the official Stephen King web presence, p. 16; Courtesy of the Official Web site of the State of Maine, p. 34; Courtesy of the Secretary of State Kids' Page, p. 31; Courtesy of the U.S. Senate Web site, p. 35; Courtesy of the University of Maine, p. 37; Courtesy of Wildblueberries.com, p. 28; *Dictionary of American Portraits,* Dover Publications, Inc., © 1967, p. 42; Enslow Publishers, Inc., p. 1; Library of Congress, p. 3 (Constitution); National Archives, pp. 36, 40; U.S. Forest Service, p. 26.

Cover Photo: ©1999 PhotoDisc, Inc.

Contents

	Report Links	4
	Maine Facts	10
1	The State of Maine	11
2	Land and Climate	18
3	Economy	25
4	Government	31
5	History	39
	Chapter Notes	46
	Further Reading	47
	Index	48

About MyReportLinks.com Books

MyReportLinks.com Books
Great Books, Great Links, Great for Research!

MyReportLinks.com Books present the information you need to learn about your report subject. In addition, they show you where to go on the Internet for more information. The pre-evaluated Report Links that back up this book are kept up to date on **www.myreportlinks.com**. With the purchase of a MyReportLinks.com Books title, you and your library gain access to the Report Links that specifically back up that book. The Report Links save hours of research time and link to dozens—even hundreds—of Web sites, source documents, and photos related to your report topic.

Please see "To Our Readers" on the Copyright page for important information about this book, the MyReportLinks.com Books Web site, and the Report Links that back up this book.

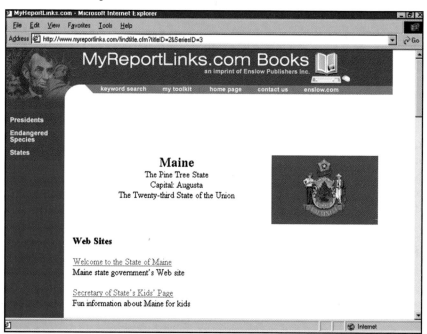

Access:

The Publisher will provide access to the Report Links that back up this book and will try to keep these Report Links up to date on our Web site for three years from the book's first publication date. Please enter **SME1641** if asked for a password.

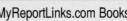

Tools Search Notes Discuss

Report Links

 The Internet sites described below can be accessed at
http://www.myreportlinks.com

▶**Welcome to the State of Maine** *Editor's choice
This wide-ranging site has information on Maine's communities, government, businesses (including agriculture and industry), economy, education, environment, arts, and recreation opportunities.

Link to this Internet site from http://www.myreportlinks.com

▶**Secretary of State's Kids' Page** *Editor's choice
There are great games here, as well as facts about Maine's government and how it works, how a bill becomes a law, famous Mainers, kids' books about Maine, and lots more. Shockwave and speakers are needed to access much of the site.

Link to this Internet site from http://www.myreportlinks.com

▶**Project Puffin** *Editor's choice
Puffins are not currently an endangered species, but they are rare in Maine. Take an interactive tour to learn more about puffins and other birds and animals found in Maine.

Link to this Internet site from http://www.myreportlinks.com

▶**Mt. Katahdin** *Editor's choice
Mount Katahdin, in Baxter State Park, is where the Appalachian Trail ends. The park offers many year-round outdoor activities. All the information you need to plan a visit to Baxter is here. Plus you will find some great Maine links!

Link to this Internet site from http://www.myreportlinks.com

▶**Get Real, Get Maine** *Editor's choice
This colorful site tells how to find real Maine food and farm products. It also has links to the Department of Agriculture, agricultural fairs, farms, and a clickable county map.

Link to this Internet site from http://www.myreportlinks.com

▶**Acadia National Park** *Editor's choice
Find out about the natural and cultural history of Acadia National Park.

Link to this Internet site from http://www.myreportlinks.com

Any comments? Contact us: **comments@myreportlinks.com**

Report Links

> The Internet sites described below can be accessed at
> http://www.myreportlinks.com

▶ Bangor, Maine
This site about Bangor, Maine, gives a detailed history, news, and information about Bangor sites and happenings. It also provides many photographs and links.

Link to this Internet site from http://www.myreportlinks.com

▶ The Center for Maine History
Portland's Center for Maine History is made up of three closely related institutions. Its Web site provides a comprehensive overview of what these institutions have to offer, as well as a tour of a past exhibition entitled "Rum, Riot, and Reform."

Link to this Internet site from http://www.myreportlinks.com

▶ Connect Maine
This site offers Maine facts, a business directory to Maine products, and links to town Web sites. Plus users are able to browse many different regions of Maine quickly.

Link to this Internet site from http://www.myreportlinks.com

▶ Explore the States: Maine
America's Story from America's Library, a Library of Congress Web site explores the state of Maine, the twenty-third state to join the Union. Here you will find basic facts and links to additional stories about Maine.

Link to this Internet site from http://www.myreportlinks.com

▶ Gulf of Maine Aquarium
To better understand the close relationship between Maine and its people and the sea, we recommend a visit to this site. During your virtual tour of the aquarium, you will learn a lot about ocean life, including marine mammals.

Link to this Internet site from http://www.myreportlinks.com

▶ Katahdin Area Chamber of Commerce
The Katahdin region of Maine encompasses many counties, towns, and Baxter State Park. This diverse region offers year-round activities and events. The Web site provides information on traveling to and through this beautiful region no matter the season.

Link to this Internet site from http://www.myreportlinks.com

Any comments? Contact us: **comments@myreportlinks.com**

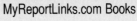

Tools　Search　Notes　Discuss　　　　　　　　　　　　　　　　Go!

Report Links

 The Internet sites described below can be accessed at
http://www.myreportlinks.com

▶ The Kennebunkport Historical Society
Find out about Kennebunkport's history and its attractions at this Kennebunkport Historical Society site. Click on "Things to Do" to visit some of this Maine village's oldest structures, including a one-room schoolhouse.

Link to this Internet site from http://www.myreportlinks.com

▶ The Land of Wild Blueberries
Most of the United States' wild blueberries are grown in Maine. This site goes into detail about the benefits of blueberries, how to grow and harvest them, recipes, and interesting facts.

Link to this Internet site from http://www.myreportlinks.com

▶ Lighthouses of Maine
More than sixty lighthouses stand guard along Maine's rocky coast, alerting mariners to dangers ahead. Take a virtual tour of some of the most famous lighthouses, including Portland Head and West Quoddy Head.

Link to this Internet site from http://www.myreportlinks.com

▶ The Maine Attraction
The official home page of Maine's Office of Tourism is a great tool for planning a visit Down East. Get started at the Regions page, which outlines the eight major tourism regions of the state.

Link to this Internet site from http://www.myreportlinks.com

▶ Maine Audubon Society
The Maine Audubon Society Web site provides information about Maine's wildlife, and wildlife and nature conservation.

Link to this Internet site from http://www.myreportlinks.com

▶ Maine Department of Economic and Community Development
Maine's Department of Economic and Community Development Web site explores such subjects as doing business in Maine, visiting Maine, and helping Maine's communities thrive.

Link to this Internet site from http://www.myreportlinks.com

Any comments? Contact us: **comments@myreportlinks.com**　7

Report Links

The Internet sites described below can be accessed at
http://www.myreportlinks.com

▶ **Maine Folklife Center**
The Maine Folklife Center boasts one of the nation's foremost collections of oral histories, music, and photographs documenting life in New England.

Link to this Internet site from http://www.myreportlinks.com

▶ **Maine Loggers**
The lumber industry has always been an important element of Maine's economy. A great page for kids with useful links to logging around the country.

Link to this Internet site from http://www.myreportlinks.com

▶ **Maine Resource Guide**
This site is a guide to Maine's tourist attractions, including all of the state's major travel destinations. You will find lots of advice on exploring the state, outdoor activities, weather, and a calendar of events.

Link to this Internet site from http://www.myreportlinks.com

▶ **The Maine Rivers Site**
Rivers have always been important to Maine's economy and history. The Maine Rivers Site offers current information on conserving Maine's wildlife and waterways for future generations.

Link to this Internet site from http://www.myreportlinks.com

▶ **MaineToday.com: Press Herald Online**
This site offers the online versions of three major Maine newspapers and one television station. It is a great resource for the latest news and events around the state.

Link to this Internet site from http://www.myreportlinks.com

▶ **Ski Maine**
Winter is Maine's longest season. With its diverse geography, the state is a premiere location for skiing and other winter sports. Skiing is a major part of Maine's tourism industry.

Link to this Internet site from http://www.myreportlinks.com

Any comments? Contact us: **comments@myreportlinks.com**

MyReportLinks.com Books

Tools   Search   Notes   Discuss   Go!

Report Links

 The Internet sites described below can be accessed at
http://www.myreportlinks.com

▶**St. Croix River**
The St. Croix River has been important in both United States and Canadian history. This site offers insights into its historical and modern-day implications for both nations.

Link to this Internet site from http://www.myreportlinks.com

▶**Stately Knowledge: Maine**
At this Web site you will find facts and figures about the state of Maine. You will also find links to encyclopedias and almanacs about Maine, as well as other useful links.

Link to this Internet site from http://www.myreportlinks.com

▶**Stephen King**
Stephen King, a well-known horror and suspense fiction writer, has spent much of his life in Maine. His official Web site offers bibliographies, a biography, a lengthy Q&A page, and excerpts from upcoming books.

Link to this Internet site from http://www.myreportlinks.com

▶**University of Maine System**
Seven universities dotted around the state make up the University of Maine system, which serves some thirty thousand students. Visit this site for an overview of the system as well as access to the sites of its individual universities.

Link to this Internet site from http://www.myreportlinks.com

▶**The United States Senate**
This site offers information on the United States government, and provides an opportunity for students to learn more about their state's senators. You will find profiles on Maine's current senators as well.

Link to this Internet site from http://www.myreportlinks.com

▶**50 States.com**
This site provides facts about Maine and all the United States. You will find state mottoes and birds, pictures of state flags, histories, and more. Each fact links to more information about each topic.

Link to this Internet site from http://www.myreportlinks.com

Any comments? Contact us: **comments@myreportlinks.com**

Maine Facts

▶ **Capital**
Augusta

▶ **Population**
1,274,923*

▶ **Bird**
Chickadee

▶ **Tree**
Eastern white pine

▶ **Flower**
White pine tassel and cone

▶ **Animal**
Moose

▶ **Fish**
Landlocked salmon

▶ **Gemstone**
Tourmaline

▶ **Insect**
Honeybee

▶ **Song**
"State of Maine Song" by Roger Vinton Snow

▶ **Motto**
Dirigo (Latin for "I lead.")

▶ **Gained Statehood**
March 15, 1820

▶ **Flag**
The coat of arms appears against a blue background. (The blue matches the shade in the United States flag). The coat of arms features a fisherman, farmer, moose, pine tree, the North Star, and the state motto "*Dirigo*."

▶ **Nicknames**
The Pine Tree State; Vacationland

*Population reflects the 2000 census.

Chapter 1 ▶

The State of Maine

Maine is a state with great natural beauty and an interesting history. It is the largest of the six New England states. Maine's Aroostook County is the biggest county east of the Mississippi River. It is so large that the states of Connecticut and Rhode Island put together could fit inside that one county. Yet only 1.2 million people live in

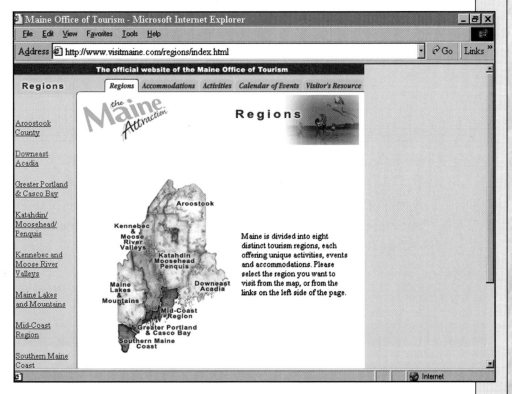

▲ Maine is the largest of the six New England states. Its sixteen counties are divided into five regions, full of diverse natural beauty.

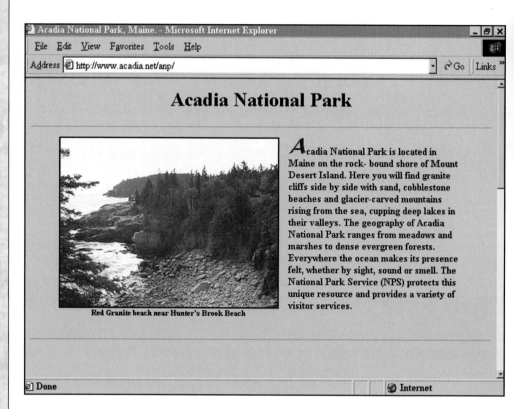

▲ Acadia National Park is the second most visited national park in America.

the entire state. More than three times that amount live in Connecticut and Rhode Island.

▶ The Great Outdoors

Unlike other eastern seaboard states, much of Maine remains undeveloped. With 17 million acres of forest, it is the most heavily forested state in the continental United States. Moose, white-tailed deer, coyotes, black bears, foxes, fishers, martens, and beavers live in these woods.

For those who love the outdoors, there is a lot to see and do. Acadia National Park, on the coast, is the second-most-visited national park in America. It boasts mountains to climb, islands to explore, and rivers and oceans to boat on or swim in. Seals, whales, puffins, and bald eagles call Acadia home.

Another natural treasure is Baxter State Park. It was named for Percival Baxter, a former governor of Maine. Baxter bought more than 200,000 remote acres in the center of the state. In 1931, he began donating this land to the people with the condition that it must always remain wild. Many people visit Baxter State Park to climb mile-high Mount Katahdin, the tallest mountain in the state. The top of Katahdin is the northern end of the Appalachian Trail. This hiking trail runs through the mountains all the way down the East Coast. It ends in Georgia.

▲ The moose, Maine's state animal, is abundant in Baxter State Park.

"Down East"

Residents of the coastal town of Eastport see the sun rise each morning before anyone else in the United States. Eastport is the easternmost point on U.S. soil. In the 1800s, sailors sailing to Maine from Boston said they were headed "down east." The name stuck. People refer to the Maine coast as Down East.

Maine was important in early American history. As early as A.D. 1000, Vikings from Scandinavia led by Leif Ericson explored the New England coast. Settlers from Great Britain and France colonized Maine in the early 1600s. In 1641, the settlement of York became the first European city in the New World.

Many miles of inlets and bays border the Atlantic Ocean. If you could stretch the coast into a straight line, it would reach all the way across the country. The state has a rich history of sailing and shipbuilding. After Americans won their independence in the Revolutionary War (1775–82), they began to build boats. Sailors and sea captains departed from Maine ports for destinations all over the world. Although the days of

One of Maine's most important exports is lobster.

tall wooden sailing ships are now past, Maine continues its tradition of shipbuilding.

When people think of Maine, they often think of lobster. Millions of pounds of lobster are harvested there each year. Today, lobster is considered an expensive delicacy. There was a time, though, when only people who could not afford anything else would eat lobster. Times have changed. Now no summer trip to the state is complete without a lobster meal. Even Maine's McDonald's fast-food restaurants serve a real lobster roll.

An Inspiring State

Maine has inspired many people to put a pen to paper. E. B. White, the author of the well-loved favorite *Charlotte's Web,* lived on a coastal farm. Robert McCloskey, a children's picture-book author, wrote such stories as *Blueberries for Sal* and *One Morning in Maine* about life on the islands off the state's coast. Stephen King, the best-selling horror author, writes in Bangor. He lives in a mansion surrounded by an iron fence decorated with cobwebs and bats. Maine-born poet Henry Wadsworth Longfellow was very popular in the 1800s. Through his poetry he recorded stories of early American life. One of his most famous poems tells the tale of Paul Revere's ride to spread the news that the British were coming.

Sarah Orne Jewett was a writer in the late 1800s. She showed the world that the lives of rural people were important.[1] The great American thinker Henry David Thoreau explored the state several times. He died in 1862 while writing a book called *The Maine Woods.* In the 1920s, a poet from Gardiner named Edwin Arlington Robinson became well known. Robinson won the Pulitzer Prize three times for his poetry.

Rachel Carson was an important environmentalist who cared about the future of the earth. She wrote the book *Silent Spring* from her house in West Southport. In it, she talked about the effects chemicals have on nature. She warned that if humans continued to use chemicals thoughtlessly, songbirds would become extinct. Her research helped to ban the use of certain chemicals. A wildlife sanctuary on the southern coast has been named in her memory.

The Maine shores and woodlands have also inspired visual artists. Winslow Homer painted watercolors of people struggling with nature. He spent the last twenty years of his life, from 1890–1910, in Prouts Neck. There

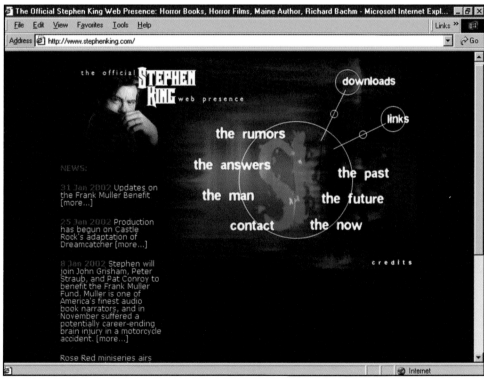

▲ Maine resident Stephen King is widely considered to be one of the best horror and suspense writers.

he created his well-known paintings of the seacoast. Artist Marsden Hartley was born in Lewiston in 1877. He became a painter of landscapes, depicting Mount Katahdin and other natural wonders. Illustrator N. C. Wyeth spent summers with his family in Port Clyde. His son Andrew grew up to be a painter. Much of Andrew's work captures rural Maine life in the 1900s. After World War I, many artists spent their summers at the beach resort town of Ogunquit. The town became an artists' colony, attracting the painter Georgia O'Keeffe, among others.

The people of Maine take great pride in their state. They have much to be proud of, even aside from the natural splendor and rich history. In 1999, the nationwide Children's Advocacy Council declared Maine the best state to raise children in. Juvenile crime is low, a high percentage of children finish high school, and few Maine children live in poverty.[2]

Chapter 2 ▶

Land and Climate

All states in the continental United States except Maine are bordered by at least two other states. Maine is more remote from its United States neighbors. Only New Hampshire touches Maine in the southwest. To the north are two Canadian provinces: Quebec and New Brunswick. Waterways play an important role in forming the boundaries. The Atlantic Ocean is Maine's eastern border. The St. John

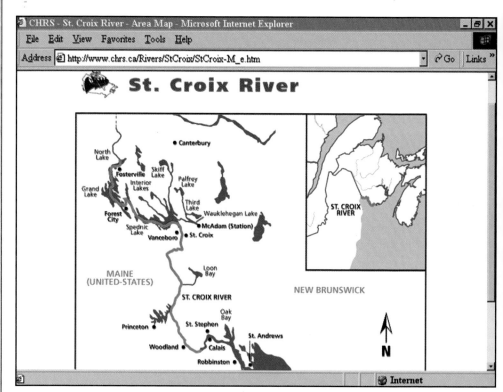

▲ The St. Croix River forms the boundary between Maine and New Brunswick, Canada.

and St. Croix rivers separate Maine from Canada. Entering the state on the highway from the south, you cross the broad Piscataqua River.

▶ A Cooler Climate

There are three different climate zones within Maine's borders. These are the coastal, northern interior, and southern interior zones. The coastal zone runs in a thin strip along the seacoast. Its average temperature is 46°F. The weather is cooler in the summer and warmer in the winter than it is in the interior. The ocean makes the climate milder. It also brings heavy fog and the occasional nor'easter. A nor'easter is a type of storm that sweeps in off the sea, bringing high winds and rain, sleet, or snow.

Maine's highest elevations are found in the northern interior zone. This region covers sixty percent of the state. The average temperature is the coldest in the state, at 40°F. The northern interior zone gets the most snow of all the zones. The southern interior zone is a bit warmer, with an average temperature of 44°F.

Maine has four distinct seasons. Winters are cold and snowy, and temperatures often fall below zero. White flakes of snow can begin to fall as early as October. It is late April before the last of it melts away with the warmer spring weather. Spring is also known by some other names: mud season or black-fly season. All the melting snow makes for a lot of mud. In rural areas, many driveways and roads are made of dirt. Driving through the spring mud can be hard work. The black fly, a small insect that gives an itchy bite, is common in the spring. These pesky insects can make enjoying the spring weather uncomfortable unless you are prepared. A hat, bug spray, long sleeves, and pants keep the bugs from biting.

▲ *During the summer months, many Mainers spend time in their "camps," or cottages, built near the water.*

Summers are comfortable. The average temperature in summer is 70°F. There is little need for air conditioners. Homes are more commonly equipped with wood stoves to take off the winter chill. Many Mainers spend time in the summer at their camps. Camps are seasonal cottages usually built near the water.

In autumn, tourists called "leaf peepers" travel far and wide to enjoy the changing colors of the leaves. As the colder weather approaches, many trees lose their leaves to prepare for winter. Before the leaves fall, they turn from green to shades of red, orange, and yellow. The hillsides are covered with breathtaking color. The glorious color is even more special because it is short-lived. Within a few weeks the wind and rain knock the leaves to the ground.

Landscape and Waterways

Maine's landscape was formed during the last Ice Age. Glaciers are made of fallen snow that, over many years, compresses into large, thickened ice masses. Because of their mass, glaciers flow like very slow rivers. These glaciers covered the land for thousands of years. Close to ten thousand years ago, the ice began to melt. The released water rushed into the ocean, causing the sea levels to rise. The higher water levels flooded the coast, drowning the land. Only the tops of the highest hills stayed above the water. The tops of those drowned hills form the 4,600 islands off Maine's coast. People live year round on some of the bigger islands. Others are home only to seabirds or seals.

The glaciers had many other effects on the land. Today, Maine's topsoil is very rocky. Topsoil is the top, rich layer of dirt that plants grow in. The weighty glaciers pressed down upon the earth, scraping the ground as they moved. When the ice retreated, the dirt and rocks that

▲ The glaciers that formed Maine's lakes and rivers left rocky topsoil that can make farming difficult.

▲ Maine has about six thousand freshwater lakes and streams.

had been caught up in the ice were left behind. Farmers still spend time picking rocks out of their fields before they can plant.

One look at a map of Maine reveals a land covered with lakes and ponds. Many of the six thousand freshwater bodies are also the result of melting ice. Some glacial melt water did not make it as far as the ocean. It settled into depressions in the ground. One special type of glacial pond is called a kettle pond. Kettle ponds were formed when a chunk of ice that was buried under the soil finally melted, leaving a deep hole in the ground.

The landscape varies greatly in different parts of the state. Sandy beaches run along the southern coast. Summer vacationers enjoy the seashore in resort towns such as Ogunquit and Kennebunk. Former-President George Bush keeps a summer home in Kennebunkport. Farther along the shore, toward New Brunswick, Canada, scenic rocky cliffs replace the sandy beaches. Small fishing villages dot the coastline. Blueberry fields cover the hillsides.

Away from the ocean, the land changes. In western Maine, mountains rise up around lakes and ponds. Sea breezes are replaced by fresh mountain air. In the north the land flattens out. Here are wide fields of potato crops. When the potato plants bloom, these fields become a sea of white flowers. Trees are everywhere in the state. Ninety percent of Maine is covered by forest.

▶ The Importance of Rivers

Rivers have played an important role in Maine's history. European adventurers used rivers to explore the inland parts of the state. They sailed upstream on the Saco, Androscoggin, Kennebec, and Penobscot rivers. People settled along the riverbanks and built villages there. They

▲ *Many vacationers come to enjoy Maine's sandy beaches in towns such as York (pictured), Ogunquit, and Kennebunkport.*

used the water as we now use highways. Boating up and down, they visited and traded supplies with neighboring villages. In the winter, when the rivers froze over, horse-drawn sleighs carried folks along the ice. Fish from the rivers provided food all year round. When industry came, people built dams that used the rivers' currents to power the mills. Two remote Maine rivers flow north toward Canada. These are the Allagash and the St. John. The U.S. government protects a corridor of land around the Allagash. By protecting the river from development, people hope to keep this beautiful area wild for future generations to enjoy. The Allagash Wilderness Waterway is a popular spot for canoeing.

Chapter 3

Economy

The valuable products of the land and waters are called natural resources. Mainers have always relied on their state's plentiful natural resources. Maine's early American Indian tribes, the MicMac and Wabanaki, lived off the land completely. For food, they collected berries, plants, and nuts; they hunted animals and caught fish. Their homes were wigwams made of wood and animal skins. The natives made blankets and clothes from animal skins and furs.

▶ Many Uses for Trees, Fish, and Animals

When the British first came to Maine in the early 1600s, they were looking for ways to increase their wealth. Sailors found a land with abundant tall, straight pine trees. The British king claimed the best of these trees as his own. The majestic pines were chopped down and shipped back to Britain, where they were used as ships' masts. Later, Americans began to build their own wooden ships. Along the riverbanks, mills were built to process the timber. Forests rang out with the sound of the lumberjacks' axes and saws. Men called river drivers floated the logs downstream to the mills. The mill workers sawed them into boards. At the shipyards, the wood was used to build ships.

Trees, fish, and animals were important resources for the early European settlers. They cleared trees from the land to build gardens and pastures for their livestock. With the logs, they built houses and boats. Fish and deer provided meat for their dinner tables. Trappers made a living by capturing animals for their fur. Beavers, foxes, weasels, and raccoons were popular fur animals. The pelts were traded to people who used them to make warm hats and coats.

Before refrigerators, people used iceboxes to keep their food cold. Once the rivers had frozen solid several feet deep, crews of men cut the ice into blocks with special saws. The blocks were then stored in sawdust inside large icehouses on the banks of the rivers. When the rivers thawed, seagoing vessels came upstream to pick up the ice. The boats delivered ice to people all over the world.

Natural resources are still an important source of jobs today. Trees are used for housing, furniture, firewood, Christmas trees, and paper products. Loggers work in the forests cutting trees down. Other people drive the freshly cut logs to lumberyards and mills. The mills convert the logs to wood and paper products. People work to keep the forests healthy by planting new trees.

▲ *Men called river drivers floated logs downstream from the forests to the mills.*

Fishing is another important industry with a long history. Fish have been an important food source as long as people have lived in Maine. Today the state harvests the most lobster in the country. Ocean fish and shellfish are also taken from the coastal waters. While some of the catch is sold locally, much of it is shipped to markets around the nation and around the world.

Industry

Many people are employed in manufacturing in Maine. Early mills made textiles (fabrics), paper, and leather goods. Mills that make wood products such as paper and toothpicks are still common in Maine today. Most other types of manufacturing have moved to areas where people will work for less money. Shipbuilding continues to be an important part of Maine's industry. One of the largest employers in the state today is Bath Iron Works. They build missile carriers and other seafaring vessels for the U.S. military.

Farming is a small but essential part of the economy. Aroostook County, for example, is famous for its potatoes. The rich soil of the St. John River valley is well suited for growing this root vegetable. Some potatoes go directly to markets for sale. Other potatoes are processed in factories to make french fries, potato chips, and hash browns. Still others are used as seed potatoes for next year's crop. Farmers plant these potatoes as seeds in the spring.

The wild lowbush blueberry is a native plant that thrives in poor soil. Almost all of the wild blueberries grown in the United States come from Maine. The blueberry bushes also add to the beautiful colors of a Maine autumn, turning a vibrant red. Fiddlehead ferns are a less well-known native crop. They are the coiled young leaves of

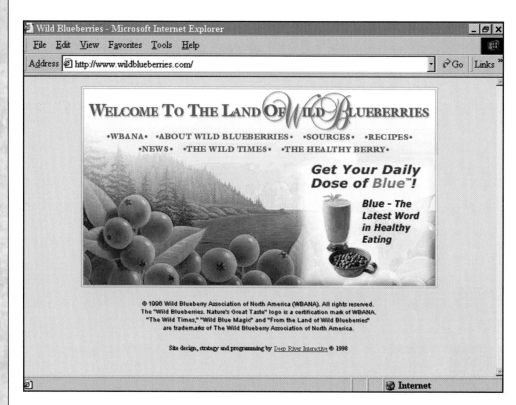

▲ Wild lowbush blueberries thrive in poor soil. Most of the wild blueberries grown in the United States come from Maine.

a fern, before it has opened. These tasty green delicacies are found in the woods in spring. Wilton, Maine, is the only place in the world where fiddleheads are canned.

▶ "The Way Life Should Be"

Maine has a tradition of quality higher education. There are excellent private colleges like Bowdoin, Bates, and Colby. The University of Maine system has campuses all over the state. Yet there are not enough jobs in Maine for everyone who needs one. Many educated young adults leave the state to find work. They look for jobs in cities to the south such as Boston and New York. With computers changing the ways people work, Mainers are hopeful that their state can attract more businesses. Maine was the first state to connect all public schools and libraries to the Internet.[1] Portland, the largest city, has already begun to see new industry start to grow.

A sign on the Maine Turnpike reads, MAINE—THE WAY LIFE SHOULD BE. Life moves at a slow pace there—just what many vacationers are looking for. License plates tout the state nickname, "Vacationland." Maine's rugged beauty attracts people who like outdoor adventure. Summer tourists kayak and white-water raft on the Kennebec, Dead,

▲ Many people travel to "Vacationland" in the winter to ski its many mountains.

and Penobscot rivers. Hikers climb mountains. In the winter, downhill skiing is a popular sport, and there are many places in Maine to ski. Two of the larger ski resorts are Bethel's Sunday River and Sugarloaf in Carrabassett Valley. They have slopes for skiing and snowboarding as well as trails for cross-country skiing.

Snowmobiling and ice fishing are other winter hobbies. Snowmobile trails zigzag all across the state. When the lakes and rivers freeze, people are able to drive snowmobiles and trucks out onto the thick ice. By drilling holes in the ice, fishermen can catch fish even in the deep winter.

Other people come to Maine to get away from the bustling crowds of big cities. In the summer, tourists enjoy the seacoast. Whether sailing, swimming, or creating sand castles on the beach, people relax to the sound of the waves. Shoppers love to spend time at the factory outlet stores in Freeport and Kittery. Freeport is best known for the L. L. Bean store. Leon L. Bean opened his business in 1905, selling a new kind of boot. His "Bean boots" were designed to hold up in all kinds of weather. Over the years, his outdoor products grew in popularity. Now the store is open twenty-four hours a day, every day of the year.

Chapter 4 ▶

Government

European settlers first came to live in Maine in the 1600s. Yet when the colonies won the American Revolution in 1776, Maine did not become a state right away. It remained a territory—no longer of England, but of the state of Massachusetts. Maine broke away, and on March 15, 1820, became the twenty-third state in the Union. Citizens met in Portland to talk about how they would

▲ Maine's state government is modeled after the United States federal government.

▲ Maine's state flag features the coat of arms on a blue background. A moose, pine tree, farmer, fisherman, and the North Star are all part of the coat of arms.

govern their new state. They looked to the United States federal government as a guide. They wrote down their decisions in a document called the state constitution. This constitution established a structure for the new government.

The state constitution splits the power between three branches of government. This guarantees that no branch can become too powerful. The three branches are the executive, the legislative, and the judicial. The governor holds the authority of the executive branch. The governor's job is to uphold the law. A statewide election is held every four years to choose a governor. A governor may serve for only two terms.

The legislative branch is made up of two "houses." The lower house is called the House of Representatives. The upper house is called the Senate. People who serve in the legislative branch are called legislators. Legislators are in charge of making the laws. Legislators who are elected to serve in the lower house are representatives. Those who are elected to serve in the upper house are senators. There are 151 members of the House of Representatives and thirty-five members of the Senate. Mainers vote for legislators every two years. The third branch is the judicial branch, or the court system. The courts interpret the law. The highest court in the state is the Supreme Court.

The People's Government

Government is not limited to the state capital of Augusta. Mainers practice democracy at a local level, too. Many of Maine's citizens attend town meetings. At a town meeting, people talk about their concerns. They work together to resolve problems that face their communities. Many people eagerly await the annual town meetings in the spring. After a long winter, it is a chance to visit with their neighbors.

The state is divided into sixteen counties. The counties are composed of twenty-two cities, hundreds of towns,

Augusta, Maine's capital, is located on the Kennebec River.

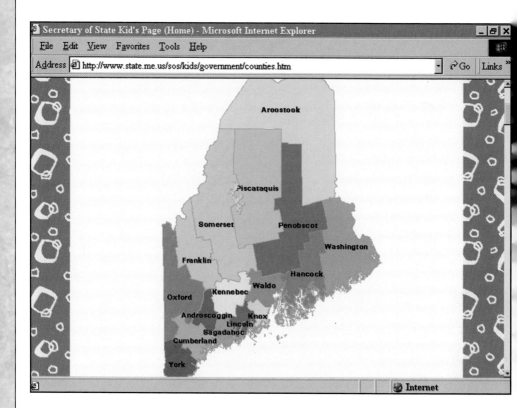

▲ Each of Maine's sixteen counties contributes to the state government in Augusta.

and three American Indian reservations. The counties also contain parcels of land that have no form of local government. These are called unorganized territories, plantations, and townships. Nearly half the state is made up of unorganized areas.

In 1974, Mainers elected James B. Longley to be their governor. Governor Longley was neither a Republican nor a Democrat. He was an Independent. This means he was not associated with any political party. Never before had a state elected an Independent governor. Independent voters continue to play an important part in Maine politics. There are more Independent voters registered in Maine than either Republicans or Democrats.[1] In 1994, Mainers chose another Independent candidate, Angus King, Jr., to be governor.

Noteworthy Politicians

Maine has produced several famous politicians. Hannibal Hamlin was vice president under Abraham Lincoln from 1861 through 1864. Like many people in the North, Hamlin felt strongly that slavery was wrong. He did not think the United States should allow slavery. In April 1861, the North and South fought the Civil War over the slavery issue, as well as other issues. Two years later, Lincoln issued

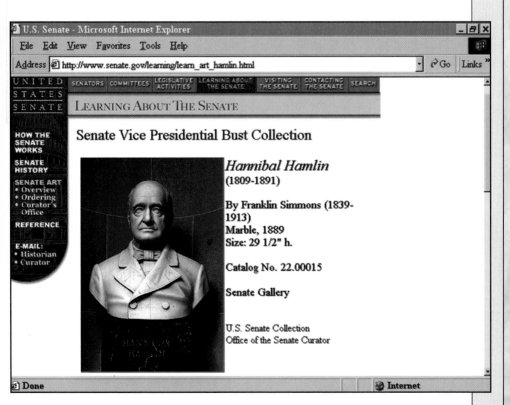

▲ Abraham Lincoln's first vice president, Hannibal Hamlin, was from Maine.

the Emancipation Proclamation that abolished slavery in the Confederate States of America. Although Lincoln was elected to another term in office in 1864, Hamlin did not stay in Washington. He may have lost popularity because he outlawed alcohol in the Senate.[2] The Republican Party chose Andrew Johnson from Tennessee to serve as vice president for Lincoln's second term. When Lincoln was assassinated a few months later, Johnson became president.

Margaret Chase Smith was born in Skowhegan in 1897. She married a local politician named Clyde Smith. In 1930, he was elected to serve in the House of Representatives, so the Smiths moved to Washington, D.C. Clyde was still in office when he died of a heart attack ten years later. Before he died, he asked Margaret to run for his seat in the House to carry on his work. At that time, women politicians were uncommon. Not only did Margaret win the seat, she also earned many people's respect with her hard work. She served for four terms in the House. In 1947, she won a seat in the Senate. No woman had ever been elected to the Senate before. In 1964, she became the first woman to seek the Republican presidential nomination. Although she lost the nomination to another candidate, Margaret Chase Smith will be remembered for paving the way for women politicians of the future.

Edmund Muskie is credited with giving the Democratic Party a voice in Maine. The son of Polish immigrants, Muskie grew up in

◀ In 1947, Margaret Chase Smith became the first woman elected to the U.S. Senate.

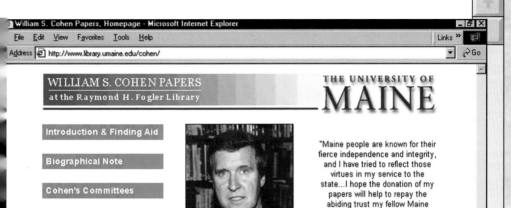

▲ William Cohen became the U.S. secretary of defense under President Clinton.

the mill town of Rumford. He did well in school and became an excellent public speaker. In 1954, he became the first Democratic governor elected in Maine in twenty years. In 1958, he was elected to the Senate, where he served for twenty-two years. Presidential candidate Hubert H. Humphrey chose Muskie to be his running mate in the 1968 election. They lost to Richard Nixon and Spiro Agnew. In 1980, President Carter chose Muskie to serve as secretary of state.

Two men from Maine played important roles in national politics during the 1990s. William Cohen was

born in Bangor in 1940. He represented Maine in both the U.S. House of Representatives and the Senate. In 1997, President Clinton chose Senator Cohen to become the secretary of defense. George Mitchell is a lawyer from Waterville. He served in the U.S. Senate for fifteen years, from 1979 through 1994. In 1988, he became Senate Majority Leader. During President Clinton's time in office, Mitchell continued to work in politics. He worked to promote peace between the Irish and the British in Northern Ireland.

Chapter 5

History

When explorer Leif Ericson came to the New England coast around A.D. 1000, he was probably looking for timber. He lived in Greenland, where there were not many trees. Nearly five hundred years later, the English, Spanish, and French sailed to the New World. The first explorers, like Christopher Columbus, were looking for a passageway to India. Instead they discovered a new land. There were stories that the New World was a place of great riches. Sailors dreamed of finding jewels, furs, and other treasures that would make them wealthy men.

Leif Ericson and the Vikings were the first Europeans to see Maine. However, they were not the first people in North America. American Indians of the Wabanaki tribe already inhabited Maine. The word "Wabanaki" means easterners, or people of the dawn. Even before the Wabanaki, people had lived in North America for thousands of years.

Not much is known about the earliest inhabitants, but they did leave some clues. Burial mounds have been found in Maine that date back to 3000 B.C. The graves contain a bright red clay. It is thought that these people used the paint during burial ceremonies. Other early peoples lived close to the coast. They left huge heaps of oyster shells, three stories tall.

▶ French and English Settlers

In 1498, John Cabot and his son, Sebastian, sailed along the Maine coast. They claimed the land as the property of

the king of England. In 1524, the explorer Giovanni da Verrazano claimed Maine for France. Over the next 250 years, both France and England considered Maine to be their territory. People from both countries crossed the ocean to live in Maine.

The first settlers to arrive were the French, in 1604. They formed a colony at the mouth of the St. Croix River. They were unprepared for the harsh winters. After several years, they gave up and went back to France. In 1607, two ships from England landed farther south, near present-day Phippsburg. The ships carried British settlers, and they built the Fort Popham colony. The British also found the winter very difficult. When the spring came, many of the settlers had died. The rest sailed back home.

More settlers followed. They had learned from the others and were better prepared. Along with the settlers, the French sent missionaries to the New World. These missionaries were Catholic priests, or abbés. They converted the American Indians and taught them Catholicism. The British settlers were not interested in sharing their religion with the American Indians. They wanted to use the land for their own settlements. The American Indians and the British often fought over the right to use the land.

During the Revolutionary War, Benedict Arnold marched 1,000 Patriot troops from Boston to Quebec to fight the British. In Maine, Arnold lost half his men to starvation and cold.

War Breaks Out

In 1675, King Philip's War broke out. This was the beginning of nearly one hundred years of war between the British and the French. Each country wanted to establish its ownership of the New World. The American Indians often sided with the French. Through warfare and disease, the American Indian population grew smaller and smaller. In 1763, the English won the final battle. Maine was declared British territory. Even so, French language and culture continue in Maine today.

In the 1770s, British settlers in all the American colonies grew angry with England. The king kept raising their taxes. They did not think it was fair to pay taxes to a faraway king, and they decided to fight for their independence. Some of the settlers, called Tories, remained loyal to the king. This was the start of the Revolutionary War.

The first naval battle of the war took place off the coast of Maine in 1775. That same year, Benedict Arnold led a group of American soldiers through Maine. His plan was to capture the British cities of Quebec and Montreal. The soldiers paddled up the Kennebec River in small wooden boats called bateaux. They marched through thick woods and soggy bogs. It was a rough trip. Their food supplies went bad. The men were so hungry they ate shoe leather. The attempt to capture the British in Quebec failed, but in the end the Americans won the war. The United States of America was born.

Becoming Maine

Maine remained a territory of Massachusetts until 1820. Then, the people of Missouri asked that their territory become a state. Slavery was legal in the territory of Missouri. At the time Missouri asked to be admitted to the

Union, there were an equal number of free states and slave states. The Northern states, which did not allow slavery, did not want another slave state brought into the Union. But the South did not want another free state admitted to the Union. Congress struck a bargain between North and South. They agreed to add two states to the Union. Missouri would become a state that allowed slavery, and Maine would be a state where slavery was illegal. With one new slave state and one new free state admitted at the same time, the balance of slave and free states was maintained. The bargain was called the Missouri Compromise.

In 1839, Mainers became upset about the boundary between Maine and New Brunswick, Canada. The governor of Maine declared war against England since Canada was under English rule. The war was known as the Aroostook War. The boundary was agreed upon before any battles were fought. Never before and never since has an individual state declared war on a nation.

Maine played an important role in the Civil War. Many people in the North felt that slavery was wrong and had to end. These people were called abolitionists. Harriet Beecher Stowe was an abolitionist who lived in Brunswick, Maine. In 1851, Stowe wrote a book against slavery called *Uncle Tom's Cabin*. Many Americans read her book and agreed that something

Harriet Beecher Stowe was an abolitionist who lived in New Brunswick, Maine, in the 1850s. Her book *Uncle Tom's Cabin* inspired many people to fight against slavery.

▲ *Industrialist John D. Rockefeller used some of his fortune to preserve the rugged Maine coastline for future generations. In 1921, Acadia National Park was founded thanks to funding from Rockefeller and others.*

had to be done. The Southern states did not want the North telling them what was right or wrong, though. They decided to separate from the North and form their own government. When the Civil War broke out, 72,000 soldiers from the state of Maine went to fight. One of these soldiers was Joshua Chamberlain. He became a hero at the Battle of Gettysburg, leading the 20th Maine Infantry Regiment. He and his men played a vital role in winning the battle by successfully defending a hill called Little Round Top. Chamberlain returned to Maine after the North won the war to serve as governor from 1867 to 1871.

A Popular Place to Visit

In the late 1800s, Maine became a popular destination for tourists. Wealthy city folks built mansions along the coast. The millionaire John D. Rockefeller was one of them. He used his wealth to preserve some of Maine's rugged coastline. Acadia National Park, established in the 1920s, was made possible through donations by Rockefeller and other wealthy visitors.

Despite increased tourism, the year-round population of Maine decreased in the twentieth century. It became more and more difficult for people to make a living from a family farm or fishing business. Large companies, aided

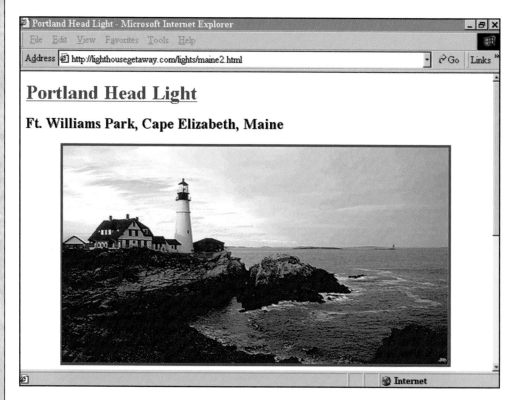

▲ Mainers hope to keep their state a beautiful place to live, visit, and work for many years to come.

by machines and technology, moved into the farming and fishing industries. Some Mainers went west in search of better land to farm. Others moved to Boston or New York in search of work. In the 1980s, the economy began to improve and there were more jobs. Now, at the beginning of the twenty-first century, computer technologies are bringing new types of jobs to Maine. The state's rich natural resources continue to provide work opportunities as well. By protecting these resources, the people of Maine hope to keep their state a beautiful place to live and visit for many years to come.

Chapter Notes

Chapter 1. The State of Maine

1. Jeff Fischer, ed., *Maine Speaks: An Anthology of Maine Literature* (Brunswick, Maine: Maine Writers and Publishers Alliance, 1989), p. 450.

2. Angus S. King, Jr., "The Best Place to Raise Children," *A Big Honor*, n.d., <http://www.state.me.us/employee/governor/thebest.htm> (April 16, 2001).

Chapter 3. Economy

1. Office of the Governor, "Road Speeches and Statements on Top Issues," *State of Maine*, n.d., <http://www.state.me.us/governor/policy/index.html> (April 16, 2001).

Chapter 4. Government

1. Jim Brunelle, "All About Maine: Detailed History," *Secretary of State's Kids' Page*, n.d., <http://www.state.me.us/sos/kids/allabout/historydetail.htm> (April 16, 2001).

2. Herb Adams and Tom Verde, *Maine's Claim to Fame: A Gallery of Personalities* (Augusta, Maine: Maine Department of Education, 1990), p. 4.

Further Reading

Aylesworth, Thomas G. and Virginia L. Aylesworth. *Northern New England: Maine, New Hampshire, Vermont.* Broomall, Pa.: Chelsea House, 1990.

Beem, Edgar Allen. *Maine: The Spirit of America.* New York: Harry N. Abrams, Inc., 2000.

Capstone Press, Geography Department Staff. *Maine.* Danbury, Conn.: Children's Press, 1997.

Cayford, John E. *Maine's Hall of Fame.* Bangor, Maine: Cay-Bel Publishing Company, 1987.

Fradin, Dennis B. *Maine—From Sea to Shining Sea.* Danbury, Conn.: Children's Press, 1995.

Gould, Alberta. *First Lady in the Senate: A Life of Margaret Chase Smith.* Mount Desert, Maine: Windswept House Publishers, 1990.

Kavanagh, James. *Maine Trees & Wildflowers.* Blaine, Wash.: Waterford Press, Limited, 1998.

Kent, Deborah. *Maine.* 2nd ed. Danbury, Conn.: Children's Press, 1999.

Kress, Stephen W. as told to Pete Salmansohn. *Project Puffin: How We Brought Puffins Back to Egg Rock.* Gardiner, Maine: Tilbury House, 1997.

Kummer, Patricia K. *Maine.* Minnetonka, Minn.: Bridgestone Books, 1998.

Marsh, Carole. *Maine Government!: The Cornerstone of Everyday Life in Our State!* Peachtree City, Ga.: Gallopade International Publishing Group, 1996.

Murphy, Jim. *Into the Deep Forest: With Henry David Thoreau.* New York: Houghton Mifflin Company, 1995.

Thompson, Kathleen. *Maine.* Orlando, Fla.: Raintree Steck-Vaughn, 1996.

Index

A
Acadia National Park, 12, 44
American Indians, 25, 39
Aroostook War, 42
artists, 16–17
Augusta, Maine (capital), 33
authors, 15–16, 42

B
Baxter State Park, 13
blueberry crops, 27–28

C
Cabot, John, 39–40
Cabot, Sebastian, 39–40
Canada, 18–19, 23, 43
Chamberlain, Joshua, 43
climate, 19–20, 40
Cohen, William, 37–38
colony of Great Britain, 41
counties of Maine, 33–34

D
diet, 15, 25

E
economy, 25–30, 45
education, 28–29
Ericson, Leif, 14, 39

F
fiddlehead ferns, 27–28
Fort Popham Colony, 40
France claims Maine, 40

G
gains statehood, 31
geography, 18–24
    beaches and coast, 14, 18, 22–23, 39
    inlets, bays, and ocean, 14, 22–23
    islands, 21
    kettle ponds and lakes, 22
    mountains and cliffs, 13, 23
    rivers, 19, 23–24
    soil, 21
    woodlands (forest), 12, 25
glaciers, 21–22
government, state, 31–38

I
industry, 24, 27–28
    farming, 23, 27–28, 45
    fishing, 23, 27, 45
    lobster, 15, 27
    logging, 25–26
    mills, 26
    shipbuilding, 14–15, 25, 27
    tourism, 15, 29–30, 44
    trapping, 25–26

K
Kennebec River, 23, 29, 41
King, Jr., Gov. Angus, 35
King Philip's War, 41

L
Longley, Gov. James B., 34

M
Mitchell, George, 38
Mount Katahdin, 13
Muskie, Edmund, 36–37

N
natural resources, 25–27, 45
nickname, 29

P
Penobscot River, 23, 30
population, 11, 44

R
recreation, 24
    camps, 20
    canoeing, kayaking, and rafting, 24, 29–30
    hiking, 30
    outdoor sports, 30
    resort towns, 22–23
    sailing, 14–15, 30
    swimming, 30
    winter sports, 29–30
Revolutionary War, 14, 31, 41

S
St. Croix River, 19, 40
St. John River, 18, 24
Smith, Margaret Chase, 36
state constitution, 32
Stowe, Harriet Beecher, 42

T
technology, 29, 45

V
Verrazano, Giovanni da, 40

W
wildlife, 12, 24, 25